MODERN RETRO

EASY HOME STYLE

Contents

Introduction

Modern retro. It's modern. And it's retro. If such a divine jumble of old and new is not an excuse for creative freedom then we don't know what is.

Modern style is associated with simplicity, minimalism and elegance – not too much clutter and a nice fresh palette with plenty of light. Retro on the other hand is richer, warmer and brimming with unexpected colours, patterns, textures and trinkets. Bringing the two together gives the home stylist a great opportunity to be inspired by both the past and the present in creating their dream home. Pretty much anything goes in the modern retro style, which makes it ideally suited to free-thinking, creative spirits who struggle with de-cluttering. One of the best aspects of modern retro is that it can be mixed and matched, or applied to varying degrees – a little or a lot – to suit your tastes.

Remember: everything old is new again!

THE VIBE

ECLECTIC

OLD AND NEW

ICONIC

GREEN

COLOURFUL

WARM

TOP 10 DESIGN ELEMENTS

1.

Wood detailing

Plentiful use of wood in floorings, on walls or in furniture adds style, warmth and comfort to the modern-retro theme. Here, the distinct geometrical pattern enhances the modern-retro vibe and makes a strong style statement that says both modern retro and earthy. You can tone it up, like this, or introduce wooden elements in furniture or photo frames for a softer look. Dark timbers, such as walnut, create an authentic look and blonder woods feel more contemporary.

2.

Retro accessories

For the modern-retro look it's important to accessorise confidently rather than going for a minimalist approach. Use retro-looking pots for flowers and plants (sourced from bric-a-brac markets or op shops) and keep your eyes peeled for quality retro mugs, bowls and other decorative objects that you like the look of. If you keep accessories to two or three colours, you'll prevent your room from looking too busy.

3.

Strong colour

Where modern retro differs most from other styles currently in vogue is in its joyful embrace of bold colour. So if you love colour, this may well be the style for you. It's all about strong, bright and earthy tones, such as mustard, gold, blue, olive, sienna, orange, teal, red and chocolate. Black and white is often used in geometric contrast, or to offset bold colours. If you are new to bold colours, start small with accessories or experiment with a feature wall.

4.

Shapes and patterns

Straight lines and corners are inevitable in the design and construction of houses. Mid-century designers softened this by the introduction of curves, circles and multiple angles in furniture and furnishings – think round coffee table or moulded chair. This added variety and warmth, as did the approach to patterns which was bold and graphic in nature. Whether geometrical (zigzags, chevrons or diamonds), graphic (dots, dashes and circles) or tribal, confident use of patterns is key to the modern-retro style. Bringing shapes and patterns together is a fun way to make a mid-century stamp on your home.

5.

Nostalgia items

Modern-retro style is full of heart and soul, and that's one of the reasons why it's so beloved by its followers. One of the best things is that you can – indeed, must – include your personal memorabilia, family heirlooms, old photographs and grandparents' crystal glasses in your styling. Nostalgia items are both free and fundamental to the modern-retro style.

6.

Select retro centrepieces

While the modern-retro look can be built largely around existing home furnishings and furniture, if budget allows consider splashing out on a piece of furniture that can act as an anchor point for the overall look. This will ensure your home looks more modern retro than mish mash. A centrepiece might be a classic Eames-style armchair, an occasional chair or a set of mid-century dining chairs. Whether original or reproduction, these pieces of furniture will help you make a definitive modern-retro style statement.

7.

Combining materials

Because modern retro combines design styles from the '50s, '60s, '70s and '80s (or earlier if you like!) it makes sense that different materials need to find a way to work together. That eclectic vibe is part of the look. Designers from the '50s onward starting using chrome, plastics, fibreglass and plywoods and new techniques allowed for moulded forms to be created from these materials. The resulting – and now iconic – curved plastic works fantastically well as a feature in the modern-retro home, and can be effectively paired with the sharper angles of contemporary furniture.

8.

Nature in every room

If indoor plants ever went out of fashion (they did in the '90s and the first decade of the twenty-first century) they are back with gusto, and they are the perfect inclusion in the modern-retro home as they bring colour, warmth and a calming energy to the home. Pretty much any kind of plant goes, but paying attention to what you display them in is key. Macrame makes a cool choice as a basket for oh-so-now hanging plants, while wooden planters are a great choice for larger plants that sit on the floor.

9.
Creating warmth

If nothing else, modern-retro style is all about creating warmth: a comfortable, comforting home environment where the family can kick back and relax together. This vibe will come together with the fusion of your existing and new style choices, but bear in mind the use of textiles and soft furnishings, such as cushions and blankets. Combining patterns and textiles from different eras can work wonderfully well to create a personal mood and that, in turn, creates warmth in the home.

10.

Borrowing from eras

Modern retro provides the opportunity to style with what you love. There are no rules about which era or what pieces go together, which spells freedom for the interior designer. Be mindful not to go overboard, however. Aim to style just two or three pieces together and try to maintain links between pieces from different eras by choosing shapes or colours that echo each other (as in the curvy shape of the candlestick and vase pictured here).

Modern-retro living spaces exude warmth and character, thanks to a personalised blend of favoured pieces of furniture and accessories. A retro statement piece can set the scene perfectly in the living room, allowing the home stylist to build the look around it – so consider investing in one if budget allows. Plenty of greenery, eclectic artwork, patterned textiles and bold colours will help build the picture. But fill the space with loved and meaningful things and you won't go far wrong in creating a space you want to come home to time and again.

This living space features key modern-retro style elements such as a retro feature lamp, a statement chair and the all-important buffet.

STATEMENT CHAIRS

A statement chair is a great way to highlight your modern-retro style. Pick your favourite style of chair and run with it. Popular statement pieces that suit the modern-retro vibe are Eames-style (moulded plywood and leather furniture popularised by Ray and Charles Eames in the 1950s) or Lloyd Loom–inspired furniture. At the turn of the 20th century, Marshall Burns Lloyd invented a loom that could weave twisted paper into a fabric partly reinforced with steel wire. This fabric, which became known as Lloyd Loom, revolutionised an area of the furniture industry and is still inspiring replica versions today (like the bucket chair pictured here).

Shades of blue bring a modern feel to this living space which features classic retro pieces such as a '60s TV and radio. Replica retro furniture brings the look bang up to date.

CERAMICS

Vases and bowls add comfort to the home and provide the perfect opportunity to accessorise with items that you love. Choose from your favourite era or materials, such as the tinted glass popular in the 1970s or the teal pottery produced in Germany in the 1960s (and pictured here), which is beloved of many retro enthusiasts. Its shiny glaze and geometric design create a look that manages to be both retro and totally 'now' at the same time.

There's something modern retro in the slope of the ceiling and window frames in this lovely living space. A low coffee table, geometric print rug and accessories cement the look.

LIGHTING

Lighting is key whatever your design style, and putting together the right mix of ceiling, pendant, desk and floor lights will help create ambience in your living room and allow you to adjust lighting to meet your requirements. Pendants are functional and decorative too. A globe-shaped pendant light as pictured here makes a bold and brilliant statement in your modern retro home. If you choose to purchase vintage pendants remember to get them fitted by an electrician, but there's no real need to go down that path when there are so many beautiful replica versions available to purchase.

Wood panelling creates warmth and a distinctly retro vibe in this home, which is complemented by a wooden dresser and ceramic sculpture.

Creating a vignette (that's a posh word for display) is a great way to create interest and personality in your room. Choose just a few items or multiple items within a theme (such as framed prints) to create a sense of cohesion.

SUBTLE CONNECTIONS

This retro-style living room brings together elements from different eras and styles, notably the Queen Anne–style antique armchair combined with a modern industrial coffee table and rustic dresser. The Persian-style rug and funky contemporary cushion also seem at odds, but the overall effect is brought together successfully by subtle connections, such as the blue in the upholstery of the chair and the rug, the studs of the chair and studded metal of the table display, and the caramel tones of the wood. The lesson when bringing elements together in your modern-retro-inspired home is to look beyond the superficial.

RUGS

Handwoven rugs and textiles complement the modern-retro look nicely, creating personality and warmth in a living room. Kilims provide the opportunity to bring the bold colours and patterns beloved of the modern-retro style into your home. Flat-woven rugs generally offer a simpler style, and more affordable option, while rag rugs have a contemporary and relaxed feel about them. At the other end of the spectrum, Persian silk rugs bring elegance to the modern-retro home. Anything goes, so choose what you love. As with most things modern retro, you can choose to buy replica versions (widely available) or the original items, which are available at specialist shops online such as Etsy.

Deep brown and black are classic modern-retro offset colours. Leather and glass add gloss and warmth to these colours.

LEATHER

This mid-century-style chrome and leather chair is a statement piece that sets the tone for any living space. A wide seat, sloping back and studded leather upholstery in black or brown tones create comfort and style in an iconic chair design of the period that has been widely reproduced.

This weathered and loved table offset by flowers in a retro blue glass vase perfectly captures the simplicity and warmth of modern retro.

DARK WALLS

Bold, striking and the perfect backdrop for artwork and plants, dark coloured walls are a modern-retro signature. If you are painting the whole room, consider using shades of your chosen colour on different walls, or just start with a feature wall. Oranges, citrus, browns, blues, blacks or yellows – all of these colours fit the modern-retro bill, and many paint companies will have ranges created to suit the period, so don't hesitate to ask about this when you are doing your paint shopping.

BOHO PENDANTS

Pendant lights made from natural fibres such as bamboo, cane or rattan are reflective of a '70s aesthetic and they work well in the modern-retro-style home, especially one with an emphasis on greenery and natural elements. Combine a pendant in this style with plenty of bushy and leafy plants such as ferns, figs and rubber plants to cement the '70s vibe.

The classic Eames chair is a fantastic statement piece, adding elegance and style to any modern-retro home.

HANGING BUBBLE CHAIR

When Finnish interior designer Eero Aarnio created
the bubble chair in 1963 he might not have believed
it would still be in demand over 50 years later. But,
why not? After all, who doesn't want to curl up into
a ball and nod off to sleep every now and again? The
original chair came on a stand but the range was quickly
complemented by a hanging version, which is still being
made today and provides for the ultimate in comfort
and modern-retro style.

CURTAINS

Window dressing is another matter of personal choice in the modern-retro home. But curtains definitely add warmth. And curtains made out of velvet add greater warmth and a sense of decadence to the home. And mustard-coloured curtains made out of velvet add a modern-retro style statement to boot.

MODERN LIGHTING

Good lighting is not confined to inside the home, nor is it necessary to stick to one style. In this modern-retro home, the exterior combines slick lines and cool materials. Spot lighting is used to illuminate the stair well and invite the visitor into the home, while flood lighting is used at the upper level to provide visibility and as a security feature. Spot lighting is used in the garden to illuminate plants and provide ambience at night time.

GROUPING IS KEY

Bringing together a few elements in a display in one area of your living room, whether it's on a coffee table, shelves or on the floor, is a job that requires a little practice but is worth the effort. A well-crafted display makes or breaks the look of a room. Bear in mind the unity/disunity rule when creating an effective modern-retro look. Here, unity is provided by the plant theme, and disunity by the diverse mix of wooden planter stand, wicker basket and terracotta pot, as well as the heights of the plants. The overall look is well-crafted and varied loveliness.

A study nook modern-retro style can be designed to accommodate feature lighting and greenery.

EATING

Open shelving is a signature of modern-retro kitchen and dining spaces. This laid-back approach allows you to put your carefully chosen kitchenware and other knick-knacks on display. (Retro kitchenware from the '50s, '60s and '70s will commonly feature in the modern-retro kitchen and dining room but it's not obligatory.) If you want to make a bold statement, consider the addition of an original retro dining table and chairs, or jumble up mismatched dining chairs to create the eclectic vibe that's key to modern-retro style.

This clean and bright kitchen borrows from the Art Deco era with its black tiling and metal stools.

RETRO KITCHENWARE

There's nothing more fun for the modern-retro enthusiast than foraging around op shops, flea markets or grandma's basement for gorgeous retro kitchenware. Whether it's Bakelite canisters, earthenware jugs and bowls, hand-stitched table linen or even a 1950s Sunbeam Mixmaster, decking out your kitchen with products from a time when quality mattered more than quantity is a sure way to bring style and good karma into your modern-retro kitchen.

Mix-and-match dining chairs are a popular style trick used by modern-retro enthusiasts. Conjuring the ecclectic vibe in a heartbeat, this approach allows you to make use of existing furniture as well as adding new pieces.

COPPER

Art Deco enthusiasts love copper, the kitchenware of choice in the 1930s and in full-swing resurgence today. Modern replicas of retro copperware are easy to come by and affordable, and provide an instant modern-retro vibe in the kitchen.

Plants looks great in a planter or pot but creative approaches like tucking them into a basket add a lovely relaxed feel.

Moulded plastic chairs are a retro classic. Pictured here is a replica of the famous 1967 Panton Chair, designed by Verner Panton, whose aim was to create a comfortable chair made in one piece that could be used anywhere. The chairs are offset here with a more contemporary style of table and bench seat.

OPEN SHELVING

Having your bits and bobs on display is a trademark of
the modern-retro style and open shelving provides a
great opportunity to showcase your favourite kitchen
items. This approach works especially well for smaller
kitchens where space is at a premium.

The combination of dark walls with open shelving and plenty of greenery sets a modern-retro tone in this cafe-style kitchen.

GOOD MORNING

POLISHED CONCRETE

Concrete flooring became the norm in the 1950s following post-war restrictions on timber. During this decade a group of mixers, including Brad Bowman, the 'father of stamped concrete', began the process of stamping concrete for decorative reasons. Concrete floors decorated with colour and patterns became popular. Today's flecked concrete floors give the nod to this era, while making a contemporary statement too.

Bold and abstract artworks with a retro touch can transform a space.

The modern-retro style is evident in all
the key elements of this dining room,
from the table and chairs to the pendant
light and the 1960s cat ornament.

COMBINING TEXTURES

Combining textures such as ceramic, wood and glass
in trademark retro colours like teal, mustard or orange
brings warmth and adds character to your dining table.
Don't forget the vintage cutlery too – easy to source
at op shops and flea markets, it adds a lovely authentic
touch to the modern-retro-style kitchen.

VINTAGE GLASSWARE

It's a wonder all those glasses have survived the years, but a rummage around op shops and flea markets will inevitably turn up some goodies. Amber coloured and embossed glassware was popular in the 1960s, while the focus in the '70s was on motifs such as flowers, swirls or other kitsch patterns. Original glassware in any style you choose (or don't be afraid to mix up colours or styles) is sure to brighten up and add soul to your kitchen.

The art of display modern-retro style is uncluttered but full with different looks and patterns incorporated.

This dining room blends chunky modern furniture with a vintage dresser and greenery at different levels used to striking effect.

OCCASIONAL CHAIRS

Occasional chairs soared in popularity during the middle of the last century, and take many forms stylistically depending on whether they were made in the '50s, '60s, '70s or '80s. Pick your style and pick your space. Occasional chairs are great for a small nook or in the corner of the room, and they can then be brought centre stage when needed for guests.

SLEEPING

In the bedroom, you can tone it up or down in terms of the modern-retro look. Cool, light colours are fine if that's your preference, while dark and moody will set the modern-retro tone more explicitly. What matters most is creating a comfortable space where you'll feel relaxed. Plants should be included if possible, as they bring soul, character (and oxygen) to the room, which will also come through in your choice of personal items to display. A deliberate retro touch can be added with a vintage-style cabinet or light fixture.

Wood panels and an iconic lamp
combine to give a classically
modern-retro feel to this bedroom.

WOODEN PANELLING

Wooden panelling was a defining feature of '50s and '60s interiors. It was often pulled down in the decades that followed, but now that it's back in vogue many designers will jump at the chance to restore it to its former glory or recreate it with original timber or veneer. The effect is a warm, calming ambience perfect for the bedroom. Note the industrial era pendant light in this bedroom that enhances the modern-retro vibe.

PLANTS IN THE BEDROOM

The modern-retro home will have plants in every room, and the bedroom is no exception. Opt for a combo of larger floor plants, such as palms, fiddleleaf figs or rubber plants, with smaller plants on display. Succulents are a great choice as they bring a contemporary vibe and require little maintenance.

This stylish bedroom embodies the boldness of the modern-retro look. Dark colours and the use of wood set the tone and the industrial-style pendant and replica '60s-style floor light are all that's needed to bring in the retro element.

DARK LINEN

The best-quality linen that you can afford is the best choice for your bedroom, as nothing says comfort and warmth more than lovely bed linen. Consider using dark colours, or one of the classic modern-retro accent colours, to enhance the mood.

This bedroom is light and bright,
with the retro styling coming into
play with the designer headboard,
pendant light and replica dresser.

VELVET STUDDED BEDHEADS

Upholstered headboards (or stuffers, as they were originally known) became popular during the 17th century, as the demand for comfort increased. The studded velvet variety had a resurgence in popularity in the '80s. Upholstered is now tipped to replace timber when it comes to bedheads, so this is a great way to add currency, cool and a touch of glamour to your bedroom in an instant.

VINTAGE RUGS

A hot tip for getting the modern-retro look is to purchase preloved floor coverings. Most rugs weren't originally mass-produced, so you can expect unique patterns and colour palettes, which bring warmth and individuality to ordinary spaces. As a bonus, you might be able to find nonstandard sizing and you can expect a high-quality product. Even if they are a little threadbare at times, not to worry, this adds style and character to your modern-retro interior.

Here the industrial look of the retro
glass and steel bedside lamp is
nicely offset by warm wood and cosy
patterned textiles.

A BIT OF BOHO

A do-it-yourself pallet bed is a great way to bring a stylish and relaxed vibe to your bedroom on a budget. Pairing with classic retro pieces such as the cabinet and vinyl record player on display here, along with plenty of greenery and lots of natural light, delivers a boho feel to this bedroom.

KIDS

Bright colours and bold patterns are signatures of modern retro that just beg to be applied to the little ones' rooms. Bringing in original items, such as crochet rugs, vintage prints or perhaps the teddy you loved as a kid, adds warmth and brings soul to their space. Likewise, an original rocking or reading chair creates a beautiful connection with the past. Teenagers may opt for a simpler interpretation of modern retro and that's fine – just one or two little touches, such as an accent colour or an artwork, are all that's required.

PATTERNS AND PATCHWORK

Modern retro's love of all things bold and beautiful
is perfectly suited to a young person's bedroom.
Regardless of gender, littlies love bright sunny colours
so incorporating them into your toddler's room via
wall or window furnishing or in accessories can work
wonderfully. Retro-style wallpaper on a feature wall
is an easy way to get the look and saves choosing,
framing and mounting a selection of artwork. Patterned
cushions and patchwork blankets are lovely items to buy
local, either from a local store or craft market.

Bedding is the perfect way to
introduce colour into your kids'
bedrooms. Be bold with linen and
bed coverings and if they, or you,
don't like it down the track then it's
easy to replace.

VINTAGE PRINTS

A feeding and reading chair is non-negotiable in a nursery, so it's a good place to start in setting the style for the room. Consider choosing a vintage print fabric for reupholstering the chair or having some comfy cushions made from your chosen print. Vintage prints of the '50s and '60s era provide great source material for this type of project, with relevant subject matter such as animals, boats or plants very common and bright colours and patterns tending to feature later on.

TEENAGERS

The older kid in your family is likely to want a more sophisticated space, and the modern-retro vibe can easily be adjusted to suit. All that's really needed for this room to complement the rest of your modern-retro-styled home is the details – the colour of cushions, choice or artwork and lighting. Here, those elements make a firm but gentle nod in the direction of a modern-retro style.

The boldness of the modern-retro style
is self evident in these two rooms with
confident choice of background colours
and art work respectively.

KEEPING IT SIMPLE

A replica retro-style bedside cabinet and anglepoise spotlight are all that's needed to suggest modern retro in this teenage girl's bedroom.

STUDY AREAS

A well-designed (and well-organised) study nook is a
nice idea to encourage your kids' efforts. Even if space
is limited, it's usually possible to create with a simple
desk and some good spotlighting to help them through
the long nights of study. A comfy chair is a must too –
and an ideal opportunity to bring an element of retro
styling to this area.

BATHING

Like the bedroom, the bathroom is a retreat of sorts, so aim to create a space where you'll love to while away some time in relaxing rituals. You don't have to renovate your bathroom to achieve the modern-retro look – it's amazing how much can be achieved by the addition of plants (and a few more plants), carefully selected bath linen and a few retro-style items on display. For a modern-retro bathroom colour scheme, you can't beat green and teal.

HANGING PLANTS

You really can't have too many plants in the modern-retro home, and the bathroom is the perfect place to show them off. In a smaller space, hanging baskets work well. Choose different styles of plant and planter to achieve the eclectic look, and complement with small plants on window sills. If you have plenty of space, a large fern or palm would also be a nice choice for the bathroom. Be as bold and unrestrained as you like.

Making green your dominant or accent colour in the bathroom is a great way to achieve the modern retro look. Go green in your tiling or cabinetry, or add elements of green in your bath linen or utensils. If you don't have room for plants, consider leaf or floral patterns in your bath linen.

VINTAGE SINKS

The cast iron vintage sink is the heartthrob of the
modern-retro bathroom – sigh. Both beautiful and
functional (with its deep recess you could pop a toddler
in there at bath time), these sinks do not come cheap
but they are widely available as replica versions. If it's a
bit out of your budget, consider playing up the chrome
and decorative mirror look in your bathroom instead.

OUTDOOR

Although it might not have been the case in the '50s or '60s, creating a lush, liveable outdoor space is just as important to today's modern-retro-styled home as to any other. Outdoor furniture will help set the mood and you can choose from sizzling retro colours to pure white, equally retro when it comes to outdoor furniture. Comfort in the form of iconic beanbags or hanging chairs will help you kick back and enjoy the view from your modern-retro-styled home.

BEANBAG

Since it first began production in Italy in 1969, the humble beanbag has become an iconic, much-loved and globally recognised piece of furniture. With the right mould-treated, water- and UV-resistant covering the beanbag is tough enough to withstand the elements, making it an outdoor furniture staple too. Comfortable, unique and low maintenance, the beanbag is an excellent choice for the modern-retro-styled backyard.

GO ACAPULCO

An innovative design in the 1950s, the Acapulco chair was originally made of vinyl cords on a metal, pear-shaped frame, and boasted ergonomic comfort and a modernist look. The original chairs would have been in vibrant colours in keeping with the era. Replica versions are available in modified styles and in more natural tones that bring a bit of the desert into your backyard. Pair with pattered cushions for maximum modern-retro oomph.

Cacti have all the quirkiness and character that's associated with the modern-retro style.

WHITE FURNITURE

It's natural to think bold colours when choosing retro-inspired furniture, but pure white has just as much impact and history to it. Back in the mid-'60s, noted outdoor-furniture designer Richard Schultz was asked by designer-goods retailer, Knoll, to create furniture that could withstand the corrosive Florida ocean air. Schultz responded with the 1966 Collection, all-white aluminium furniture, which is still in production over fifty years later. The iconic range includes adjustable and contour sun loungers (or chaises) as well as dining tables and ottomans. Rest assured: white is all right when it comes to retro-inspired outdoor furniture.

HANGING OUT

The hanging egg chair is retro royalty, thanks to
Denmark's Nanna Ditzel, who created the breakthrough
design in the late 1950s, when she released the hanging
chair in sturdy rattan material for outdoor use. The
chair has been replicated in many ways, including this
hip macrame version that suits the modern-retro style
perfectly and provides the perfects spot for hanging
out – literally.

RATTAN AND CANE

Rattan was the material of choice for outdoor (and plenty of indoor) furniture in the 1950s and it continued to be used through subsequent decades, in large part due to its durabilty. The material is also lightweight and pliable, making it relatively easy to shape into the rounded shapes popular in mid-century design. Rattan and cane look great paired with patterned cushions or squabs in bright colours to seal the modern-retro look.

THE
DETAILS

COLOURS

1. Teal

2. Sienna

3. Stone

4. Mustard

5. Coral

6. Olive

MATERIALS

1. Walnut Wood

2. Concrete

3. Moulded Plastic

4. Wood Panels

5. Brass

6. Glass

FABRICS

1. Leather

2. Wool

3. Vintage Prints

4. Mix-and-Match Patterns

5. Natural Fibres

6. Velvet

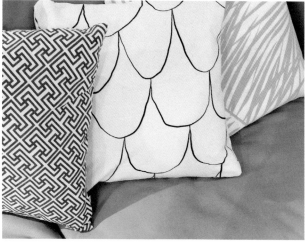
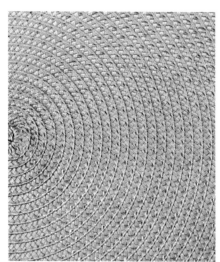

GREENERY

1. String of Pearls Plant

2. Hanging Fern

3. Rubber Plant

4. Zanzibar Gem

5. Golden Pothos

6. Snake Plant or Mother-in-Law Tongue

ACCESSORIES

1. Retro Kitchenware

2. Wooden Plant Stands

3. Angled Lightshades

4. Pendant Lights

5. Sunburst Mirrors and Clocks

6. Retro Ornaments

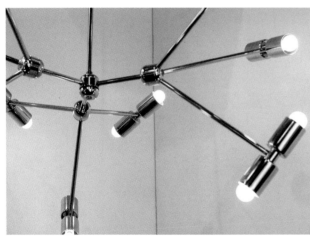

First Published in 2018 by Herron Book Distributors Pty Ltd
14 Manton St
Morningside
QLD 4170
www.herronbooks.com

Custom book production by Captain Honey Pty Ltd
12 Station Street
Bangalow
NSW 2479
www.captainhoney.com.au

Cataloguing-in-Publication. A catalogue record for this book is available from the National Library of Australia

ISBN 978-0-947163-77-8

Printed and bound in China by Shenzhen Jinhao Color Printing Co., Ltd

All images © Shutterstock except pages:
2, 39, 53,74, 78 © Kaboompics
8, 25, 37, 51, 89, 97, 99, 161, 179 © Unsplash
41, 63, 158, 164, 167, 168, 173, 174, 185 © iStock
61, 79, 170 © Austock

5 4 3 2   18 19 20 21 22